Reaching for the Nightingale

poems by

Beth Fox

Finishing Line Press
Georgetown, Kentucky

Reaching for the Nightingale

Dedicated to the next generation of the Hyde family, especially Sophia, James, Ian, Evie, Ren and Rowan. You will bring unique abilities to a world that needs your skills.

ACKNOWLEDGMENTS

Acknowledgments to the editors of pieces published elsewhere:

Basket of Going Back: *Covid Spring II*, Granite State Pandemic Poems
Swallows Over Star Island: *The Portsmouth Herald*, Portsmouth, NH
El Nino del Circuito: *The Poet's Touchstone*, Poetry Society of New
Hampshire
A Painting: The Studebaker: *The Poet's Touchstone*, Poetry Society of New
Hampshire
When the Nightingale Sings: Page Gallery Ekphrastic Pairing Contest, Poet's
Corner, Belfast, ME

Publisher: Leah Huete de Maines
Editor: Christen Kincaid
Cover Art: Brenton Hamilton
Interior Artwork: Norman Royle
Author Photo: Beth Fox
Cover Design: Elizabeth Maines McCleavy

Order online: www.finishinglinepress.com
also available on amazon.com

Author inquiries and mail orders:
Finishing Line Press
PO Box 1626
Georgetown, Kentucky 40324
USA

Contents

1.

Recipe for Loss

It's been a while.
How about we spend time this morning?

I'll make an omelet
with these black trumpet mushrooms
I found at Squam Lake yesterday—
brew spring green tea, serve peeled
peaches, blackberry jam, still warm.

Did you miss me?

You have something you always wanted.
When your back is turned, it's gone.
there is no replacing the magenta
loss of it.

Even as the green peel
slips from the cucumber,
a hare's paw clutches my jaw.

I dreamed the baby was outside
last night, all alone.

When the Nightmare Wakes Him Up

he comes to me crying, can't say what
is bothering him at first, he is shaking so.

*What will I do when my mom and dad
are gone?* he asks. I think awhile, let him
ponder his question, while I do, too.

Well, I say, *you will walk the dog like your
mother does and give him treats.*

*You will make biscuits like your dad's,
crusty on the outside, flaky on the inside*

*and you will offer them with butter
at the kitchen table. You will*

*tell your children stories, some
of the same ones that I am telling you.*

I think—
this child who makes himself heard,
          he's becoming a listener, too.

You're going to be all right,
          I tell him, and I mean it.

What a Blackberry Knows

Sun-warmed,
a berry melts bumps
of flavor on my tongue.
I am in no hurry to swallow,
replace this berry
   with another one...

Now reminds me how
each one tastes
like the first blink
   of morning,

that moment
when you wake up
and don't yet know
   how old you are.

1944: Tennessee Bride on Nantucket

At the general store, they laugh
when she asks for *sweet milk.*
What other kind is there? they say.

Why, there are all kinds.
There is sweet milk, slightly sour
milk, buttermilk, and all forms
of clabbered milk, she replies.

The milk stays sweet for a couple of days.
We used to keep it in the spring
after milking the cow,
since iihse was expensive.

Milk starting to turn- it's still good
for cooking and drinking;
as it clabbers, it becomes fermented.
When churned, it leaves thin buttermilk,
which some love; it's great for biscuits.

When it becomes very thick,
you strain out the whey, make
cottage cheese—some use the whey
but we throw it out.

And so, the bride goes back
to her second-floor apartment
with a bottle of sweet milk,
a little cream on the top,
skims it for tea.

Swallows Over Star Island

They dip and soar together
   swoop to snatch bugs
that hover in cracks
   where the ocean seeps in.

They seem to know
   their distance from others
is momentary, a space
   that doesn't matter at all.

What matters is they know
   where each swallow soul is
just like I know where
   your soul is—
      since it took flight.

Painting Days

She used to scrape and paint
my father's wooden boat,
a ketch, named Cock Robin.

A smile appeared as she worked,
her upturned gaze like a sailor
watching the sails fill.

I'm limited now...
can't do what I used to do,
she tells my youngest brother.

Straw hat bobbing,
white hair wisping,
she moves the paintbrush

back and forth,
rhythmically painting chairs
she knows will provide us rest—
the end of each summer day.

Buster

I follow Uncle Buster to his workshop.
He is holding his pipe in the palm
of his hand, clicking his lighter deftly.
A puff-puff of cherry scent causes me to
breathe deeply. It is summer vacation.
For the moment, he is all mine. I begin…

Well, I declare, says Buster,
listening to the rambling story
of a 7-year-old, as we wait for lunch.
His Tennessee drawl always captivates
me. *You don't say,* he continues, after
pausing to remove a nail from his mouth.
He always wants to hear my stories, I think.

One day he is busy in his shop
when I launch into a long one.
I'll be jiggered, he says,
 keeps working.

I repeat it to myself,
 like the way it sounds.
I'll be jiggered.
The words roll off my tongue,
easy as an insult to my brother.

I willowed out, grew long, lean.
Heard stories about Buster
and the war; he took a war bride
just before going. Now I have
two cousins, *blood sisters.*

Once, walking with a friend
in Harvard Square, half-listening,
when I said *I'll be jiggered,* I got
a look of puzzlement.

In college, I read a novel about a cattle prod
and a slave. Later, the saying became a wisp
of smoke in the air…Buster, the scent
of cherry tobacco, pipe in his hand.

When the Nightingale Sings

The real subject in poetry isn't the voice.
The real subject is silence. (Li-Young Lee)

during the night, he sings long.
I think, he must be hungry, yet
his longing sings on.

Sometimes I awake
hungry —for words,
so hungry I forget to eat.

I take two baskets,
one for peonies, a beach rose
and some lemon thyme, to see
how the light hits them.

In the other basket, I put
verbs— words of turns
rises, and strums that roll
against each other while I walk.

Like the early bird who
gets a word, I reach,
swallow whole.

More come. I catch phrases
only to let them go—
surprised when they give back
their rich silence.

After the Fourth Reading of Joy Harjo's Poem:
"For Calling the Spirit Back from Wandering the Earth in Its
Human Feet,"

>I feel a seismic shift, call my son,
>>talk about nothing and he says,
>>>*You ok, mom?*

>*Sure.* I hang up, the floor still rumbling.

I go back, read the piece again, this is number five:
>*Find your way to the circle, to the fire kept burning by*
the keepers of your soul, (where) you will be welcomed.

Ah, to just sit by the fire and stare. Release the tremblor from my
being. What would that be like? I'll read until I stop shaking—a
hundred times, if that's what it takes.

Dinner is ready. The door slams, a tremor. I'm off-balance,
>shoulders tense.
The refrigerator opens, a beer can pops, the ballgame switches on.
My body braces.

 Harjo says:
>*Let go the pain you are holding in your mind, your shoulders,*
your heart, all the way to your feet.

>Rifle sits in the corner, like an uprising in the ground. I'm a
>grandmother now. Time upended. Images still in my bones,
quivers in
>>my feet. Flashes from the past come
>>like a shot.

I want to ask my son: *Do you remember when you were locked out*
of the house bare-footed, in pajamas, in winter? ~~You talked about that~~
~~once.~~

Some earthquakes are still. The languishing of time, a quiet upheaval, stillness of not knowing. I think of Lucky, our safari guide in Zimbabwe, who no longer has work. It doesn't help to know that some are ok.

In another reading:
If you sing, it will give your spirit lift to fly to the stars' ears and back.

So, I sing. Sing a lullaby to the child that is grown, sing Amazing Grace, in all its yes, amazing forms.

A Grandson's Questions

A mild winter day, the lake draws us
to new-formed ice on the shore…

Along the path to the rise,
 foot falls in step,
the crunch of snow,
we see the expanse of ice,
hear the river flow through the dam.

With a ski pole poke of the ice
              comes a question:
Are there different kinds of ice, Umma?
   So many memories rise, like
       bubbles in the ice: Where do I begin?

There is black ice, gray ice, snow ice,
              candled ice, corn ice…
Safe ice and not so safe ice.

How do you tell?

You peer through a patch of black,
         see leaves on the sandy bottom…
test it with an ice augur, hammer and chisel.

My mind goes to winter sports,
         an accident on skis.
The one time I do not have icepicks
 I fall through…there's
         a quick rescue by two men,
                 bodies spread out
      a pair of hands pull me
voices guide me
until
         I am safe, cold
dripping, shivering.

Despite the blanket by the stove,
hot tea with sugar and milk
takes an hour to warm me.

* * *

We explore shell ice, ice stars, imagine
the depth of ice away from shore.
I save the story for another time.

When She's Missing Tennessee,

she says, *Think I'll make some cornbread.*
Out comes the worn black skillet—in goes
a spoonful of unappealing gray grease
from a can at the back of the enamel stove.

It turns gold and fragrant, specks of bacon
floating, all added to the corn meal batter
that sizzles brown around the edges in the pan,
into the oven with the brown stain at the bottom.
Soon the kitchen smells of hot bread, and a bit
of something else. It takes a while to cool, before
the crispy triangle shape appears on my plate.
Dad loves bacon; Mom loves the grease.

      In late life, they leave Cape Cod.
Dad sails his wooden ketch in the Tennessee River,
      builds Mom a pool attached to the house.

Sometimes I hear her say, *I'll make grits, or meatloaf*
with hominy, or *I'll make succotash.* I don't like lima beans,
even with corn. *Why do you put hominy in the meatloaf?*
It has no flavor. She says *the white corn hominy*
takes on the flavors of onion and spices when it cooks.
it's what you do when you make meatloaf.
I eat it. I eat the grits, too, with butter, salt, and pepper.
She smiles at me.
      After Dad dies, she moves North
takes turns living with five kids.

When she lived with me, now and then she would say,
Today I will have leftover cornbread in milk.
I used to have it in buttermilk, like your grandfather did,
but today I will have it in sweet milk.

Corn doesn't agree with me anymore,
but I can't resist a perfect cornbread—hear her voice
when I eat it, though
    I never have corn bread in cold milk.

II.

Basket for Our Times

Throw out
          those who talk to hear
              themselves talk
      the Senator who eats rutabaga every day
            the quick-bound baby and the bath
                water

          burn zombies, news,
              credit cards, flags—
          kill the cash cow

Lay in
          those who need someone
              to talk to
            everyone under thirty
              a single canvas shopping bag

          writing like your life depends on it
              a flag you create
            the baby you swaddle with your ferocity
              suckle with your sureness
      the compost of your life

          take everything out
              put only half back

Recess in Ohio, 1951

In first grade, your best friend
is the one who pushes you higher
on the swing than you ever dreamed.

Ferris Dunbar gave me the first
under-duck, propelling me skyward.
Gasping, I almost forgot to hold on.

I could feel his muscles rippling,
as he launched me faster,
and longer, leaping

from harm in time
to keep from getting winged
by that returning swing.

His toothy smile, me, thrilled.
If I forgot and screamed, the teacher
would say, *No more ducking.*

One day, after school,
he was walking home.
I called *Ferris,*

running after him. Turning
to me—he was stiff, unsmiling.
Down the unfamiliar street

I followed him, aware of
change, a darkening.
Quiet and firm-like, he said,

You better go now,
skin shining like charcoal
in a way I never noticed

before. Over his shoulder,
 I saw no swing, no yard
but a close-set row of houses

small as my kitchen. Next day
and the next, Ferris wasn't there
waiting for me to beg for

 just one more flight.

Some Questions:

After Jane Hirshfield

A frozen pond has beauty,
causes nightmares. How do you
          know the ice is safe?

                    *

What blackberries do I pick,
what hill do I climb?
               Blackberries know.

                    *

Where are you going?
 To pick honey mushrooms,
          clabber buttermilk,

find bristlecone pine trees
          on Telescope Hill,
steal some time
   under their dying branches.

                    *

Can a biscuit cure a nightmare?

                    *

A basket of apples,
          a slice of melon—
               is that a prayer?

                    *

What are questions for?

GW Carver at the Senate Hearings, 2022

Limping, in a rumpled suit, a branch
of hawthorn in his lapel, George
seats himself near the Everytown delegation,
crocheting basket in his lap. He knows long waits,
appeared before a House committee on tariffs, 1921.

Each day, he places a potted peanut plant
at the Speaker's podium, sits crocheting
listens to words the heat of violence brings,
solutions from arm the teachers to ban AR-15's.
He and his mother were taken from the Carver's
Missouri farm. An infant, only he returned,
fragile as a Hawthorn blossom. His master's wife
taught him plants, needlework. It calms him.

On the fifth day, McConnell holds up the peanut pot
quizzically. Certain he is being set up, he asks
for the gardener to rise.

**You know about plants, I take it. My wife, she
has foreign beetles on her roses. How can I kill them?**

*Plant catnip, chives, garlic, odorless marigold,
nasturtium, white geranium, rue, or tansy nearby—
they will move away.*

**And the hornworms eating her tomatoes,
the potatoes, what can I do to eradicate them?**

*Confuse the sphinx moth: plant borage,
dill and basil, wildflowers. Nurture them.*

**Ah, if she survives the poison ivy, I will do that.
Scourge of the earth, it poisons me.**

*Poison ivy, it grows in poor soil, sir.
Smother it with compost, manure
wood chips. Nearby, support jewelweed,
native wild grape, native wisteria.
Like the hawthorn, provide protection,*
            love.
                        Give the children
                                what they need.

Sometimes You Have to Go There

Chelydra Serpentina are harmless unless
provoked. They mature at twelve and
can live up to a hundred years.

It's warm already at five in the morning.
All I hear is the beep-beep of back-up
alarms, the grind of dredging and paving.

Along the rail trail that crosses the pond,
she lumbers ashore, from marshy depths,
followed by more, all digging their nests.
Glistening shells are covered with sand—
mounds contain no eggs at all. Snappers
follow their drive, glide to the shallows.

Through decayed leaves, I follow their splashes—
dive into the dimness, rest in the low light,
away from the din toward a beckoning pause,
back to the child that I was once, except I dive—
toward now, less concerned with claws.

Standing Bare, 2022

Twenty years gone,
I climb Telescope Hill again
      to see bonsai green
  in my favorite grove,
    a stand
  of bristlecone trees.

    This time,
they hang cliff-like—
their bark fogged with gray;
      flaming orange needles
      mound
    and mound
  around their storied trunks.

After thousands of years,
   these elders are needled
      by bark beetle
made strong
by the ever-brightening
  sun,

   leaving me
     to stand bare.

Ladder of Other

On the way to church Sunday
Nana turns her head
to the clink of beer bottles
at Little Creek, three fishermen
brown-bagging along the banks.

She slows the car, stares so's
they notice… and they do—
look back at the woman
in a black polka dot dress,
white hair loose in pin curls
three grandchildren dressed
their best in the back seat.

White trash! She sputters
to us. *They are worse than
poor blacks.
I caught plenty of catfish
in my day…never saw
misbehavin' at the crick.
Swan—eee.*

The anger in her words
confused me. Always
there was a pause, return
to warmth, fairness.
As a child, I did not know
of this thing called
comparing.

In that moment, my rung
on the ladder became clear,
and a world called other.
I took the first unthinking
step of many. It was
a long time before I learned
I could take the ladder down.

El Nino del Circuito

Matamoros, Mexico 2021
Population: 520,000

Except for the graffiti wall behind you,
you could be my son, Antonio. Fifteen and saucy,
thick chains of silver hanging from neck and wrist,

your head tucked under a cap too large.
Matamoros, it says, gold cascading over
a red, white, and green road, backed in black.
I see a shadow of a smile beneath its brim.

I remember when you were twelve, sleeping
on the kitchen floor, factory work in your future:
windshield wipers, gas masks: one dollar an hour.

Your Facebook occupation: smuggler.
A stealth athlete, you lead migrants thru brush
over rocks at Las Rusias; the goal, to win.
Go, Mama, Go.
In less than a minute, nine cross over,
scramble down a dirt road. You,
a hundred dollars richer for each one.
Chivos you call them: goats.

They write rap songs about you. New tattoos
line your arms. Seventeen now,
photo of you with a gun.
Will you kill for cash? You miss,
return home vomiting, dripping red.
In the night, they take you.
Three days later, you reappear,
wrists weeping from chains.

* * *

At fourteen, when the gang asked you
Will you cross the Rio Grande for money?
you didn't know what they are talking about.

Rose on the Colorado Plains

1942 Granada War Relocation Center, now
2022 Site of Natural Historic Site Act

There's a wind-tumbled
barrenness in this field
where archaeologists dig detritus—
a dented tin mug   an army surplus trench
shovel, bent—crumbling cement blocks
a bramble, just a few gnarls of green.
Can it survive?

Undesirables—
It's
our civic
duty to
take them
(Ten thousand
incarcerated)
sand of desolation
in the eyes

after
eighty years
a Day of Remembrance
at Amache Cemetery,
pilgrims gather

are greeted
by one pink bud
of Witness Rose.

To the Words in the Reflection Pool

your meanings come gently
              in your own time,
                          felt instead of heard—

you are the watering can that arcs, satisfies
              thirsty hibiscus
                          Black-eyed Susan in the sun

you are the heartbeat-pause between each note
              of the hermit thrush call, stored
                          under my breastbone

and the words of swallowtails
              on the fragrance of Korean lilac
                          in this overgrown garden

you are the stillness of red oak branches
waving to say, let go,
                          take back again

and you are the blackness
              of a long autumn night,
                          when
                          no birds call at all

Seasons, 2022

People are unmasked,
Apple blossoms in full bloom.
Can we trust this spring?

Purple as the sunrise
among brown and yellow ferns
asters line the tracks.

A shredded flag
can be repaired
by good will.

Time of Pause

We're caught in a veil of imminence.
How were we supposed to know?
On our long walk toward permanence.

We thought we'd go where we chose to go,
till this enclosed us like a heavy cloak.
We're caught in a veil of imminence,

a stream which beckons with its flow.
Beside it was a place to choose
on our long walk to permanence.

Following passions, we thought we knew.
A pause to listen helps us now:
we're caught in a veil of imminence.

The birds are calling *told you so.*
Somehow, we were supposed to know,
how to walk this walk to permanence.

Birds are calling *told you so.*
Now it seems it was all for show.
Surrounded by this imminence,
there's no such thing as permanence.

A Painting: "The Studebaker"

The old Studebaker sits
in a sagging barn,
grass creeping in to regain the floor.

Prepped for paint once, but unfinished
like hair pinned up for a canceled date,
the prom corsage going to someone else—

though clearly the car still waits
for finishing touches, pats on the seat cushions
a couple to slide in

take the long way by the river,
arrive at the dance late so the audience takes
in a red dress to match the burgundy wax

shine—class of '49
tassel hanging from the mirror.

A Melon, a Prayer

The outdoor market is dotted with little white tents
    pulsating in the breeze.
Wandering the field, my grandson asks:
   Umma, how do you know when a melon is ripe?

In an instant, I am shopping with my mother:

Like a cocker spaniel looking to settle,
   she walks around the produce display,
bent over with the intentness
   of checking my neck after the bath.

She eyes each one, gives it a thump.
         Are you round? Unblemished?
Just the right hint of yellow,
      free of light green,
    without black on the bottom?

It's my turn.
    Nodding toward the melon,
I feel its heft. To see if I can trust it—
    I let its faint aroma
   arouse my instincts, while he
  watches me with interest.

Back at the house, I will slice,
    carve and talk to cantaloupe,
      pass him a moist, inviting moon

as prayerfully as my mother would do
    and then say,

   Sometimes you just know which one to pick.

After the Pandemic: The Basket of Going Back

What to put inside?
Let's change the currency
to breath, sunshine—to the park
where a child reaches up, takes
his father's hand.

Bury old fish in the garden,
buy the market where you shop.
Take the rhyme out of the line,
and throw out the who cares.
Pound out the wise penny.

Put all empty needs
at the curb of unimportance
and pick up the basket.

With Thanks

The poetry scene in New England is extraordinary. I was blessed to take part in reading and critiquing groups, like Writers-in-the-Round on Star Island, Poetry Parlor, PORT (Poets of the Round Table), Wheaton Academy, Cook Library: Mountains Meet the Sea, Poets-in-the-Attic, Poetry Corner and Bald Poetry. There is no better way to hone your skills than to read poetry, write and share with others. Every member of these groups has enriched me.

I especially want to thank mentors Brian Evans-Jones and his poetry chapbook and publishing group, who have forever changed the way I read poetry and look at the published work of others. Reading with Brian and members of Poetry Parlor has broadened my outlook.

Kimberly Cloutier Greene, Nancy Wheaton, Barbara Bald and Bob Demaree, I thank you for your mentoring and keen comments. Ellen Bass, you and Meg Keaton are out there, building the poetry community and influencing my writing. Bob and Anne Hyde, Wayne and all my family, know that you have been with me with your example, your wisdom and your encouragement.

Beth Fox loves being connected to the arts and the community of poetry in New Hampshire. Her work is found in *The Poet's Touchstone, The Seacoast Anthology, Covid Springs II* and *the 2010 Poets Guide to NH*. A finalist in four New England contests, she helped seniors publish their work in an anthology, Other Voices, Other Lives.

Coming from a background in education, science and journalism, Beth became more drawn to poetry than ever during the pandemic. Her chapbook, *Reaching for the Nightingale*, reaches deep and far into art, culture, love, and loss during the time of Covid, when we were trying to make sense of our lives. The cover speaks to the longing she experienced when putting the collection together.
Life experiences are the subject of many poems, touching on events that have affected us deeply.

Beth has traveled extensively and loves the wild outdoors in all seasons. Often found on the water, she kayaked 35 miles on Thoreau's wilderness route in Maine. Beth loves exploring and discovering unique lives in nature, like jumping spiders and skunk cabbage. She lives in Wolfeboro.